Table of Co
Phonics
Grade 1

Review A-Z 3
Review A-Z 4
ABC Order 5
Letter Mm 6
Letter Ss 7
Letter Tt 8
Letter Hh 9
Letter Kk 10
Letter Bb 11
Letter Ff 12
Letter Gg 13
Letter Ll 14
Letter Nn 15
Beginning Consonant Dd 16
Letter Ww 17
Letter Cc 18
Letter Jj 19
Beginning Consonant Rr 20
Beginning Consonant Pp 21
Letter Vv 22
Letter Yy 23
Letter Zz 24
Letter Qq 25
Consonant Xx 26
Beginning Consonants: Bb, Cc, Dd, Ff 27
Beginning Consonants: Gg, Hh, Jj, Kk 28
Beginning Consonants: Ll, Mm, Nn, Pp 29

School Specialty
Publishing

Send all inquiries to:
School Specialty Publishing
8720 Orion Place
Columbus, OH 43240-2111

ISBN 0-7696-7621-9

1 2 3 4 5 6 7 8 9 10 WAL 09 08 07 06 05

Beginning Consonants: Qq, Rr, Ss, Tt 30
Beginning Consonants: Vv, Ww, Xx, Yy, Zz 31
Review 32
Review: Beginning Consonants 33
Review: Beginning Consonants 34
Review: Beginning Consonants 35
Review A-Z 36
Ending Consonants: k, l, p 37
Ending Consonants: g, m, n 38
Ending Consonants: r, s, t, x 39
Ending Consonant Sounds 40
Ending Consonants 41
Beginning and Ending Consonants 42
Beginning and Ending Consonants 43
Short Vowel Aa 44
Short Vowel Aa 45
Short Vowel Ii 46
Short Vowel Ii 47
Short Vowel Uu 48
Short Vowel Uu 49
Short Vowel Oo 50
Short Vowel Oo 51
Short Vowel Ee 52
Short Vowel Ee 53
Review Short Vowels: Oo, Uu, Ee 54
Short Vowels 55
Long Vowel Sounds 56
Long Vowels 57
Super Silent e 58
My Vowel List 59
Consonant Blends: sp, st, sw 60
Consonant Blends 61
Consonant Blends 62
Beginning Blends 63
Consonant Blends 64
Ending Consonant Blends: ft, lt 65
Ending Consonant Blends 66
Ending Consonant Blends 67
Ending Consonant Blends 68
Review 69
Answer Key 70-80

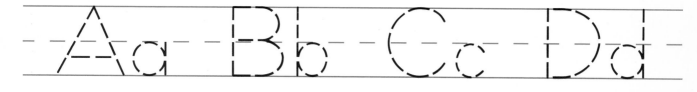 **Trace** the letters **Aa-Zz**. Then practice **writing** them on the lines below.

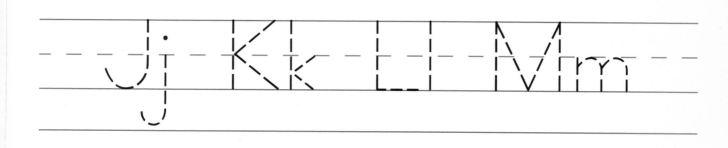

Aa Bb Cc Dd

Ee Ff Gg Hh Ii

Jj Kk Ll Mm

Review

Trace the letters **Aa-Zz**. Then practice **writing** them on the lines below.

Nn Oo Pp Qq

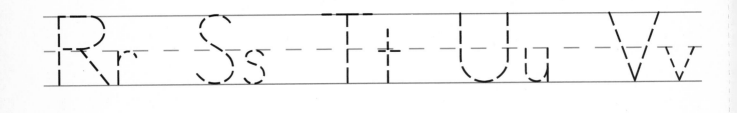

Rr Ss Tt Uu Vv

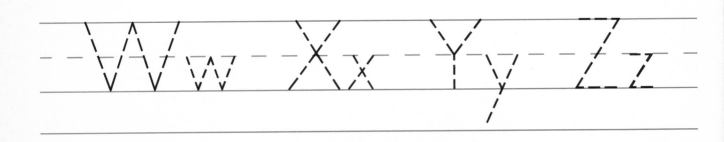

Ww Xx Yy Zz

4

ABC Order

Directions: Abc order is the order in which letters come in the alphabet. Draw a line to connect the dots. Follow the letters in **abc** order. Then color the picture.

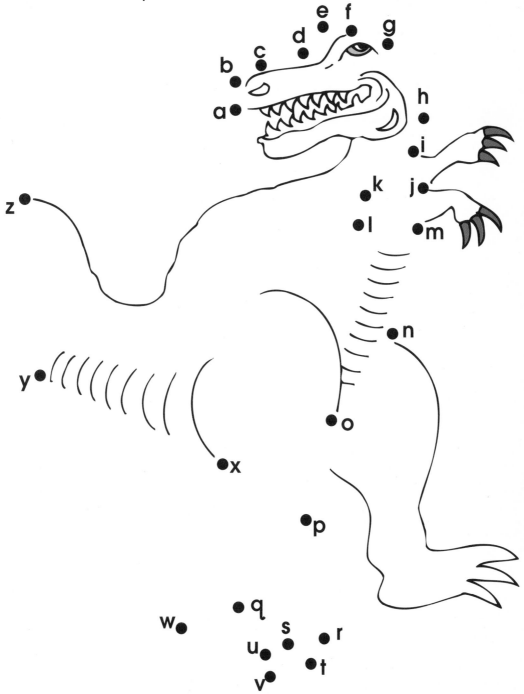

Circle the **M** or **m** in these words:

man	monkey	nest	Maria
spider	hat	flower	mask
make	bird	Martin	Mark

Circle the pictures that start with the sound of **Mm**. **Color** the pictures.

Letter Ss

✎ **Circle** the **S** or **s** in these words:

sun	see	milk	six
Sam	saw	men	sailboat
Susie	sea	silly	swan

✎ **Circle** the pictures that start with the sound of **Ss**.
Color the pictures.

Phonics: Grade 1

Color the pictures that begin with the sound of **Tt** orange. Then **color** the rest of the picture with bright colors.

8

Letter Hh

How many pictures can you find that begin with the sound of **Hh**?

Circle them! **Color** the picture!

Letter Kk

✏ **Circle** the **K** or **k** in these words:

key	kite	soda	kangaroo
Kim	cart	high	karate
toe	Kelly	art	Kevin

✏ **Circle** the pictures that start with the sound of **Kk**.
Color the pictures.

Letter Bb

Bobby Bear blows beautiful bubbles.

Color the bubbles with pictures that begin with the sound of **Bb**.

Circle the **F** or **f** in these words:

fire	Faye	took	fork
table	Fred	car	farm
Father	ten	four	fish

Circle the pictures that start with the sound of **Ff**.
Color the pictures.

Name _____

Circle the **G** or **g** in these words:

goat   Gregory   park   gate

great   tree   Gloria   gift

goose   garden   Georgia   gym

The letter **Gg** can have more than one sound. Circle the pictures that start with the sound of **Gg**. **Color** the pictures.

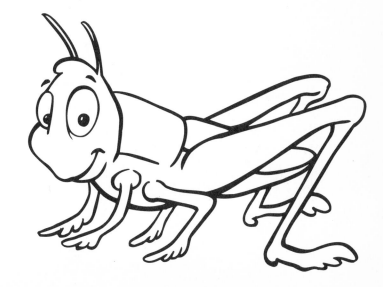

Letter

Lucy lost her luggage! Help her find it.

Color the pictures on the luggage that begin with the sound of **Ll**. Then **color** Lucy's clothes!

luggage

14

Nice Nate likes to share peanuts.

Draw a circle around each picture that begins with the sound of **Nn**. Then **color** all the pictures!

Beginning Consonant Dd

Oh, no! A **d**inosaur is at the **d**oor!

D d   **d**inosaur

Directions: Say the picture names in each box on the door. Circle the picture whose name begins with the same sound as **dinosaur**.

16   ©2006 School Specialty Publishing

Letter

Ww

✏️ **Circle** the **W** or **w** in these words:

window	Walter	walk	win
said	was	Marjorie	white
Wendy	boat	willow	want

✏️ **Circle** the pictures that start with the sound of **Ww**.
Color the pictures.

Letter
Cc

Circle the **C** or **c** in these words:

cat	Casey	ran	can
cow	corn	cup	Carol
hand	wall	crack	car

Circle the pictures that start with the sound of **Cc** .
Color the pictures.

Beginning Consonant Jj

What is Jamie wearing today?

Say each picture name.

Color the spaces whose picture names begin with the sound of **Jj blue**. **Color** the other spaces yellow.

◆ What is Jamie wearing?_____

19

Beginning Consonant Rr

Directions: Trace and write the letter Rr. Start at the dot. Say the sound the letter makes as you write it.

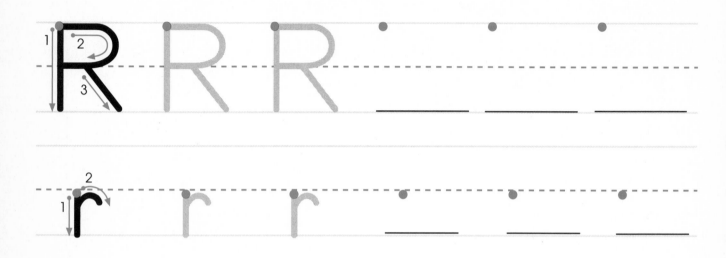

Directions: These pictures begin with the letter Rr. Color these pictures.

rabbit

rocket

ring

rake

Beginning Consonant Pp

Directions: Trace and write the letter Pp. Start at the dot. Say the sound the letter makes as you write it.

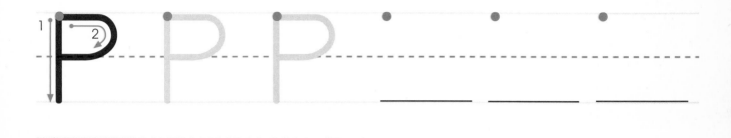

Directions: These pictures begin with the letter Pp. Color these pictures.

pin

pillow

pie

pail

Phonics: Grade 1

Help Vern Vampire vacuum.

Circle the pictures that begin with the sound of **Vv**. **Color** all the pictures.

Letter
Yy

Make this yo-yo spin.

Color only the pictures that begin with the sound of **Yy**.

Letter

Take a trip through the zoo.

Color only the pictures that begin with the sound of **Zz**.

Letter

Circle the **Q** or **q** in these words:

pop	Quincy	quarter	quilt
bike	quit	Quinn	quiet
balloon	Mary	quail	fun

Circle the pictures that start with the sound of **Qq**.
Color the pictures.

Phonics: Grade 1

Consonant Xx

Directions: Trace and write the letter Xx. Start at the dot. Say the sound the letter makes as you write it.

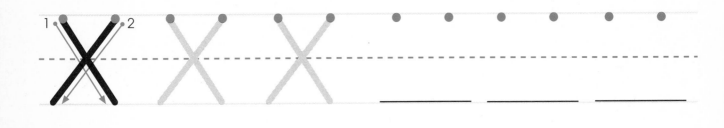

Directions: These pictures have the letter Xx in them. Color these pictures.

xylophone

exit

x ray

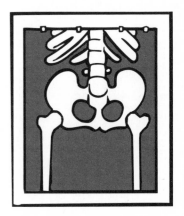

26

Beginning Consonants: Bb, Cc, Dd, Ff

Directions: Say the name of each letter. Say the sound each letter makes. Draw a line from each letter to the picture which begins with that sound.

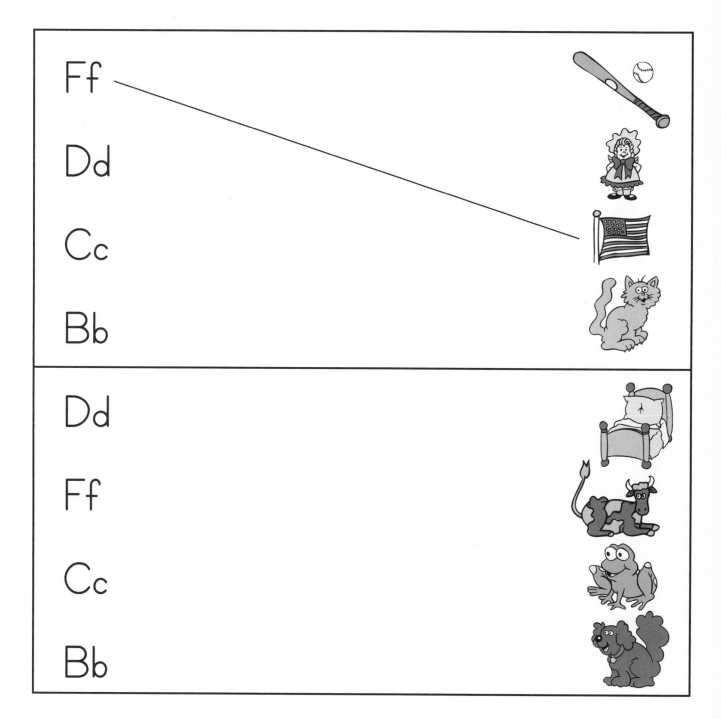

Beginning Consonants: Gg, Hh, Jj, Kk

Directions: Say the name of each letter. Say the sound each letter makes. Trace the letter pair that makes the beginning sound in each picture.

Gg   Hh   Jj   Kk

Kk   Hh

Gg   Kk

Gg   Hh

Jj   Gg

Beginning Consonants: Ll, Mm, Nn, Pp

Directions: Say the name of each letter. Say the sound each letter makes. Trace the letters. Then draw a line from each letter pair to the picture which begins with that sound.

Ll   Mm   Nn   Pp

Ll

Mm

Nn

Pp

Phonics: Grade 1

Beginning Consonants: Qq, Rr, Ss, Tt

Directions: Say the name of each letter. Say the sound each letter makes. Trace the letter pair in the boxes. Then color the picture which begins with that sound.

Beginning Consonants: Vv, Ww, Xx, Yy, Zz

Directions: Say the name of each letter. Say the sound each letter makes. Trace the letters. Then draw a line from each letter pair to the picture which begins with that sound.

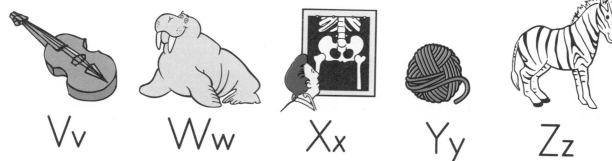

Vv   Ww   Xx   Yy   Zz

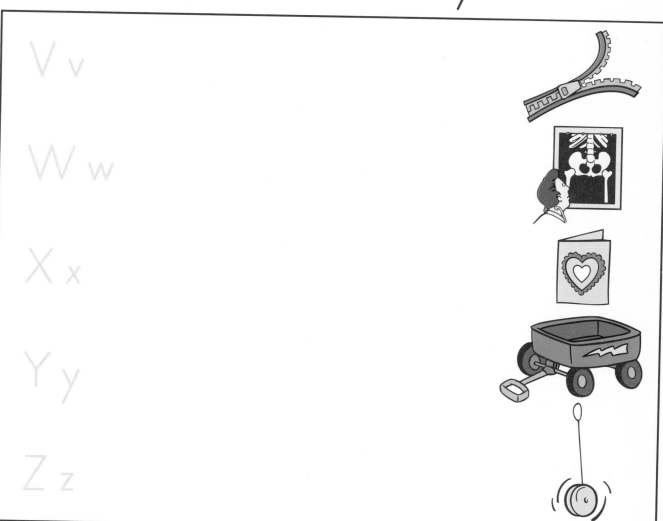

Phonics: Grade 1

Review

Directions: Help Meg, Kent and their dog, Sam, get to the magic castle. Trace each capital consonant letter and write the lower-case consonant next to it. Say the sound each consonant makes.

V_ W_ Y_ Z_
X_
T_
S_
R_ P_ M_ K_
Q_ N_ L_ J_
H_
G_
C_ F_
B_ D_

Review: Beginning Consonants

Directions: Say each picture name. Circle the letter that stands for the beginning sound.

P T	B P	N C	B T
N B	T N	T B	T P
P B	C P	C B	T C
T P	N C	N P	B P
B C	P N	C B	C T

33

Review: Beginning Consonants

Directions: Look at each picture. Say its name. Write the letter for the beginning sound in each picture.

_____   _____   _____   _____

_____   _____   _____   _____

_____   _____   _____   _____

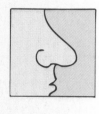         

_____   _____   _____   _____

_____   _____   _____   _____

Review: Beginning Consonants

Bb   Cc   Tt   Nn   Pp

Directions: Look at the letter at the beginning of each row. Say each picture name. Circle each picture whose name begins with the sound the letter stands for.

B				
C				
T				
N				
P				

Review A-Z

Say the name of each picture.

Write the letter that makes the beginning sound for each picture.

_____ ar

_____ ipper

_____ ite

_____ etter

_____ oat

_____ ose

_____ un

_____ ouse

_____ urtle

_____ lasses

_____ ar

_____ og

Ending Consonants: k, l, p

Directions: Trace the letters in each row. Say the name of each picture. Then color the pictures in each row which end with that sound.

37 *Phonics: Grade 1*

Ending Consonants: g, m, n

Directions: Say the name of each picture. Draw a line from each letter to the pictures which end with that sound.

g

m

n

38

Ending Consonants: r, s, t, x

Directions: Say the name of each picture. Then circle the ending sound for each picture.

 r s t x

 r s t x

 r s t x

 r s t x

 r s t x

 r s t x

 r s t x

 r s t x

Look at the picture in each box.

Circle the pictures in that row that have the same ending sound.

  10

40

Ending Consonants

 be**d**

 ba**g**

 ja**m**

Directions: Write the letter to complete each word.

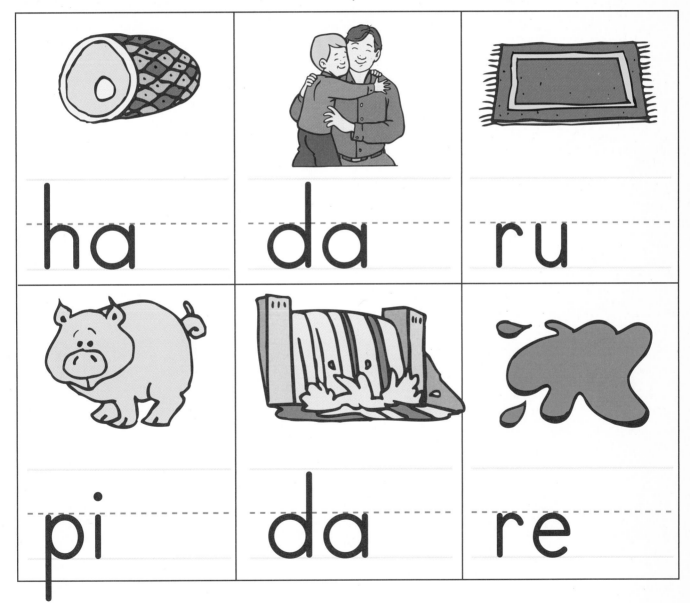

ha	da	ru
pi	da	re

Beginning and Ending Consonants

Directions: Say the name of each picture. Write the beginning and ending sounds for each picture.

_b_  _g_   ___  ___

___  ___   ___  ___

___  ___   ___  ___

___  ___   ___  ___

Beginning and Ending Consonants

Directions: Say the name of each picture. Draw a triangle around the letter that makes the **beginning** sound. Draw a square around the letter that makes the **ending** sound. Color the pictures.

o r t f d w v t b

x c r t g d d a k

l m h x g r p t v

43

Short Vowel Aa

Directions: Trace and write the letter Aa. Start at the dot. Say the sound the letter makes as you write it.

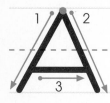

Directions: These pictures begin with the letter Aa. Color these pictures.

 apple

ant

 animals

 astronaut

Short Vowel Aa

Directions: Say each picture name. Write **a** if you hear the **short a** sound.

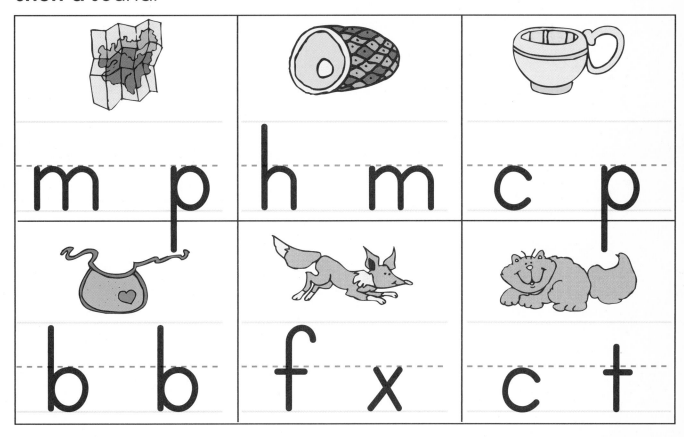

m   p   h   m   c   p

b   b   f   x   c   t

Directions: Use a toy car or pretend your finger is a car at the top of each hill. Smoothly move your finger or car down the hill as you blend the letter sounds to say the name of the picture. Then trace its name on the line.

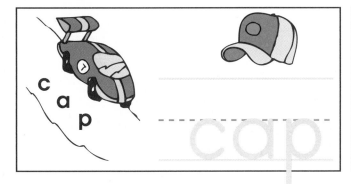

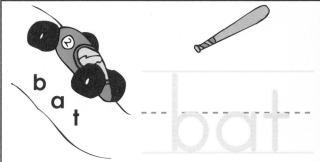

Short Vowel Ii

Directions: Trace and write the letter Ii. Start at the dot. Say the sound the letter makes as you write it.

Directions: These pictures begin with the letter Ii. Color these pictures.

ink

inch

igloo

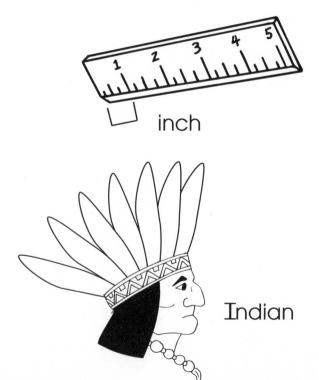

Indian

Short Vowel Ii

Directions: Blend the letter sounds to read each word. Write the word on the line.

b i b

_____

p i n

_____

Directions: Write the word that names each picture. Then find three other things in the picture whose names have the short i sound and circle them.

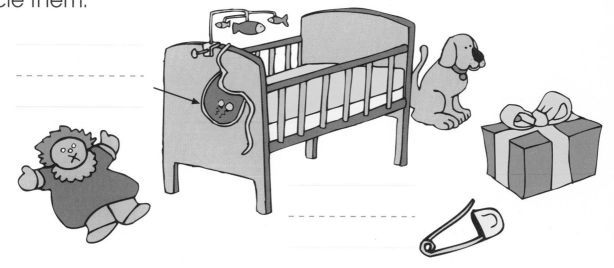

- - - - - - - - - -

- - - - - - - - - -

Short Vowel Uu

Directions: Trace and write the letter Uu. Start at the dot. Say the sound the letter makes as you write it.

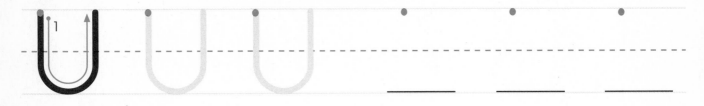

Directions: These pictures begin with the letter Uu. Color these pictures.

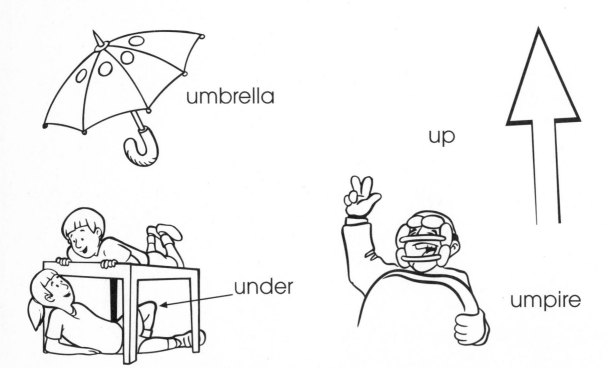

umbrella

up

under

umpire

Short Vowel Uu

Directions: Look at the pictures and read the words. Draw a line from each picture to the word that matches it.

bus

cup

gum

bug

Short Vowel Oo

Directions: Look at the pictures and read the words. Draw a line from each word to the picture which matches it.

Short Vowel Oo

Directions: Trace and write the letter Oo. Start at the dot. Say the sound the letter makes as you write it.

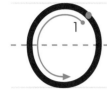

Directions: These pictures begin with the letter Oo. Color these pictures.

octopus

owl

ostrich

ox

Name_____

Short Vowel Ee

Directions: Trace and write the letter Ee. Start at the dot. Say the sound the letter makes as you write it.

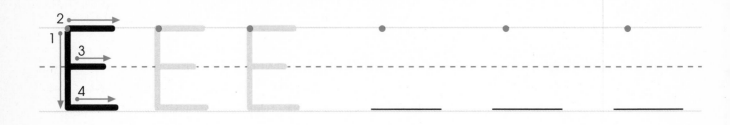

Directions: These pictures begin with the letter Ee. Color these pictures.

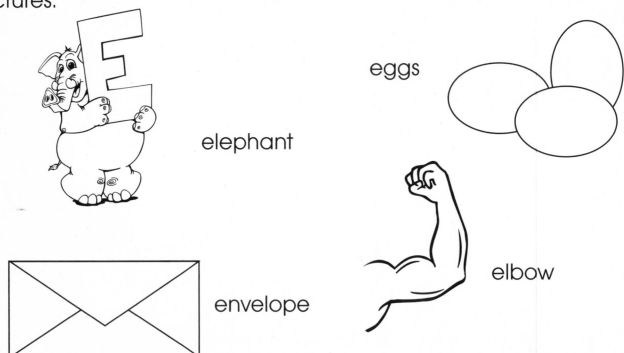

elephant

eggs

envelope

elbow

Short Vowel Ee

Directions: Say the short vowel sound for the letter Ee. Look at the pictures. Color the pictures if they begin with the sound of the short vowel Ee.

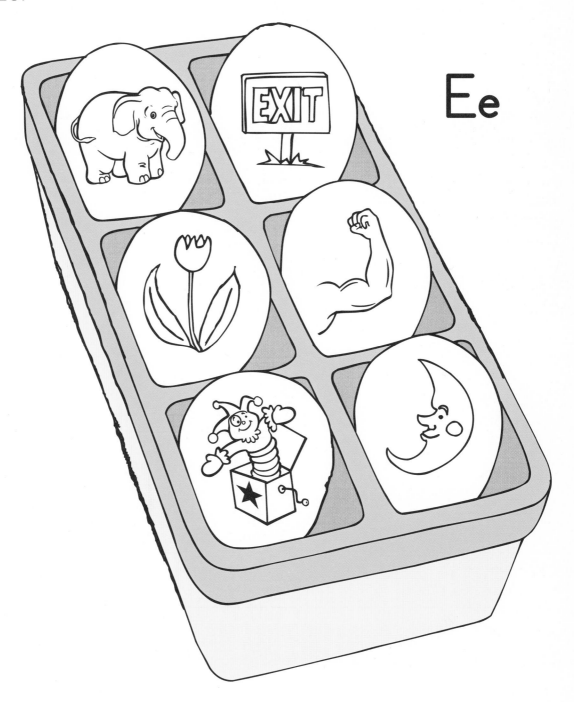

Ee

Say each picture name.

Circle the vowel sound you hear.

o u e   o u e   o u e

o u e   o u e   o u e

o u e   o u e   o u e

Short Vowels

Vowels are the letters **a**, **e**, **i**, **o** and **u**. Short **a** is the sound you hear in **ant**. Short **e** is the sound you hear in **elephant**. Short **i** is the sound you hear in **igloo**. Short **o** is the sound you hear in **octopus**. Short **u** is the sound you hear in **umbrella**.

Directions: Say the short vowel sound at the beginning of each row. Say the name of each picture. Then color the pictures which have the same short vowel sounds as that letter.

Long Vowel Sounds

Directions: Write **a, e, i, o** or **u** in each blank to finish the word. Draw a line from the word to the picture.

c ___ ke

r ___ se

k ___ te

f ___ t

m ___ le

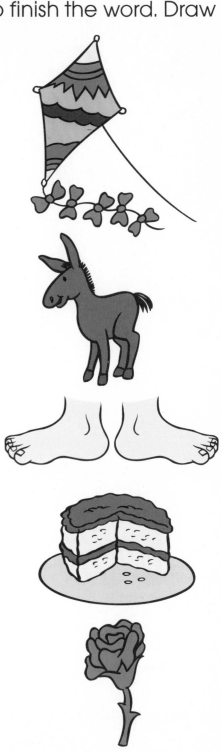

Long Vowels

Vowels are the letters **a**, **e**, **i**, **o**, and **u**. Long vowel sounds say their own names. Long **a** is the sound you hear in **hay**. Long **e** is the sound you hear in **me**. Long **i** is the sound you hear in **pie**. Long **o** is the sound you hear in **no**. Long **u** is the sound you hear in **cute**.

Say the long vowel sound at the beginning of each row. Say the name of each picture. Then **color** the pictures in each row that have the same long vowel sounds as that letter.

ā				
ē				
ī				
ō				
ū				

Phonics: Grade 1

Name _____

When you add an **e** to the end of some words, the vowel changes from a short vowel sound to a long vowel sound. **Example:** rip + **e** = ripe.

Say the word under the first picture in each pair. Then add an **e** to the word under the next picture. Say the new word.

pet _____

tub _____

man _____

kit _____

pin _____

cap _____

Keep this list handy and add more words to it.

short a
(ă as in **cat**)
_____   _____

– – – – – – – – –   – – – – – – – – –

long a
(ā as in **train**)
_____   _____

– – – – – – – – –   – – – – – – – – –

short e
(ĕ as in **get**)
_____   _____

– – – – – – – – –   – – – – – – – – –

long e
(ē as in **tree**)
_____   _____

– – – – – – – – –   – – – – – – – – –

short i
(ĭ as in **pin**)
_____   _____

– – – – – – – – –   – – – – – – – – –

long i
(ī as in **ice**)
_____   _____

– – – – – – – – –   – – – – – – – – –

short o
(ŏ as in **cot**)
_____   _____

– – – – – – – – –   – – – – – – – – –

long o
(ō as in **boat**)
_____   _____

– – – – – – – – –   – – – – – – – – –

short u
(ŭ as in **cut**)
_____   _____

– – – – – – – – –   – – – – – – – – –

long u
(ū as in **cube**)
_____   _____

– – – – – – – – –   – – – – – – – – –

Draw a line from the picture to the blend that begins its word.

sk

sl

sm

sn

sp

st

sw

Consonant Blends

Consonant blends are two or more consonant sounds together in a word. The blend is made by combining the consonant sounds.

Example: **fl**oor

Directions: The name of each picture begins with a **blend**. Circle the beginning blend for each picture.

bl   fl   cl

cl   fl   gl

fl   bl   pl

fl   cl   gl

pl   gl   cl

gl   fl   sl

gl   fl   cl

sl   fl   cl

cl   gl   sl

Consonant Blends

Directions: The beginning blend for each word is missing. Fill in the correct blend to finish the word. Draw a line from the word to the picture.

_____

- - - - - - - - - - - - - - - -
_____ ain

- - - - - - - - - - - - - - - -
_____ og

- - - - - - - - - - - - - - - -
_____ ab

- - - - - - - - - - - - - - - -
_____ um

- - - - - - - - - - - - - - - -
_____ ush

- - - - - - - - - - - - - - - -
_____ esent

Beginning Blends

Directions: Say the blend for each word as you search for it.

```
b  l  o  s  l  e  d  a  b  f  t  k  a  i  n
l  b  r  e  a  d  x  s  t  o  p  i  x  a  p
o  l  g  u  f  e  n  p  s  p  i  d  e  r  i
c  l  o  w  n  a  w  l  p  z  j  c  r  a  b
k  t  c  e  n  t  h  s  t  e  g  l  q  c  r
d  h  b  r  e  a  e  j  w  k  x  o  w  h  y
h  u  s  n  a  k  e  m  d  j  l  c  m  a  j
v  m  i  u  k  l  l  s  k  u  n  k  c  i  f
i  b  g  l  o  b  e  m  h  n  o  q  t  r  r
b  f  l  j  x  s  y  a  z  s  l  e  d  o  o
s  h  e  l  l  w  k  l  f  s  s  v  u  p  g
h  a  r  l  c  a  d  l  l  v  w  k  z  s  n
o  z  y  q  s  n  l  t  a  h  n  r  u  m  q
e  f  l  o  w  e  r  a  g  l  o  v  e  e  r
w  g  m  b  c  e  n  m  o  p  d  o  f  l  g
p  r  e  s  e  n  t  r  a  i  n  b  p  l  i
```

Words to find:

block	sled	globe	crab
clock	frog	present	flower
train	glove	skunk	snake
swan	flag	smell	spider
bread	small	chair	shell
stop	sled	shoe	
thumb	wheel	clown	

Consonant Blends

Directions: Look at the first picture in each row. Circle the pictures in the row that begin with the same sound.

Ending Consonant Blends

ft lt

✏️ **Write lt** or **ft** to complete the words.

be _____

ra _____

sa _____

qui _____

le _____

Ending Consonant Blends

Directions: Every juke box has a word ending and a list of letters. Add each of the letters to the word ending to make rhyming words.

___and

b _____

h _____

l _____

s _____

___ent

b _____

d _____

t _____

w _____

___ump

b _____

d _____

j _____

p _____

___ink

p _____

s _____

l _____

th _____

___ing

r _____

s _____

st _____

k _____

___ank

b _____

r _____

s _____

t _____

Ending Consonant Blends

Directions: Draw a line from the picture to the blend that ends the word.

lf

lk

sk

st

Ending Consonant Blends

Directions: Say the blend for each word as you search for it.

```
b  e  l  t  l  e  m  m  i  l  k  r  p
b  r  l  z  m  a  a  i  u  v  r  i  n
r  r  d  u  m  p  s  h  n  x  i  t  a
i  b  p  i  n  g  k  p  i  b  n  g  w
n  m  k  i  q  i  w  e  n  t  g  d  s
g  t  h  i  n  k  n  c  e  s  i  r  h
e  e  i  k  i  f  h  r  c  d  x  e  e
t  c  s  j  b  c  l  a  s  p  n  m  l
e  r  i  e  l  o  m  n  i  y  e  p  f
n  b  n  b  a  n  d  k  g  o  s  f  k
t  a  g  l  n  a  l  a  n  d  t  e  d
x  d  c  o  k  u  z  j  e  l  u  m  p
r  a  f  t  b  r  h  s  h  r  i  n  k
```

Words to find:

belt	raft	milk	shelf
mask	clasp	nest	band
think	went	lump	crank
ring	blank	shrink	land
bring	tent	dump	sing

Review

Directions: Finish each sentence with a word from the word box.

sting	shelf	drank	plant	stamp

1. Tom _____ his milk.

2. A bee can _____ you.

3. I put a _____ on my letter.

4. The _____ is green.

5. The book is on the _____ .

Answer Key

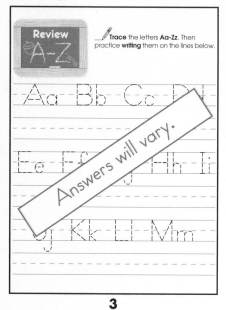

3

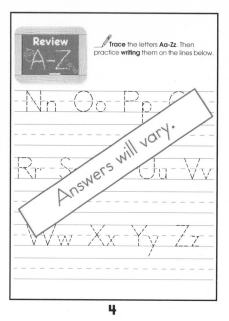

4

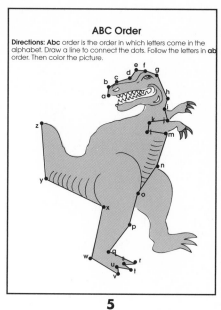

ABC Order

Directions: Abc order is the order in which letters come in the alphabet. Draw a line to connect the dots. Follow the letters in **ab** order. Then color the picture.

5

man   monkey   nest   Maria
spider   hat   flower   mask
make   bird   Martin   Mark

6

sun   see   milk   six
Sam   saw   men   sailboat
Susie   sea   silly   swan

7

8

9

key   kite   soda   kangaroo
Kim   cart   high   karate
toe   Kelly   art   Kevin

10

11

fire   Faye   took   fork
table   Fred   car   farm
Father   ten   four   fish

12

goat   Gregory   park   gate
great   tree   Gloria   gift
goose   garden   Georgia   gym

13

luggage

14

Phonics: Grade 1

15

Beginning Consonant Dd
Oh, no! A **d**inosaur is at the **d**oor!

Dd **d**inosaur

Directions: Say the picture names in each box on the door. Circle the picture whose name begins with the same sound as **dinosaur**.

16

window   Walter   walk   win
said   was   Marjorie   white
Wendy   boat   willow   want

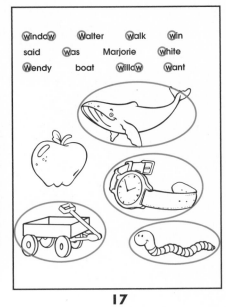

17

Cat   Casey   ran   can
Cow   Corn   Cup   Carol
hand   wall   crack   car

18

What is Jamie wearing? _____ jeans

19

Beginning Consonant Rr
Directions: Trace and write the letter Rr. Start at the dot. Say the sound the letter makes as you write it.

Directions: These pictures begin with the letter Rr. Color these pictures.

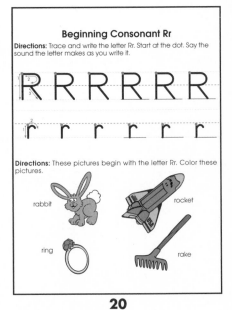

rabbit   rocket
ring   rake

20

Beginning Consonant Pp

Directions: Trace and write the letter Pp. Start at the dot. Say the sound the letter makes as you write it.

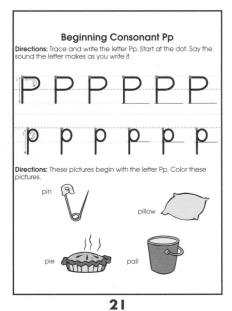

Directions: These pictures begin with the letter Pp. Color these pictures.

pin

pillow

pie

pail

21

22

23

24

pop   Quincy   quarter   quilt

bike   quit   Quinn   quiet

balloon   Mary   quail   fun

25

Consonant Xx

Directions: Trace and write the letter Xx. Start at the dot. Say the sound the letter makes as you write it.

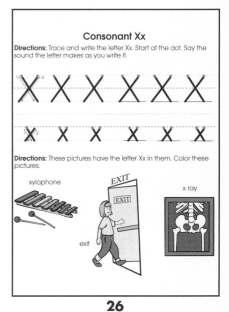

Directions: These pictures have the letter Xx in them. Color these pictures.

xylophone

EXIT

exit

x ray

26

Phonics: Grade 1

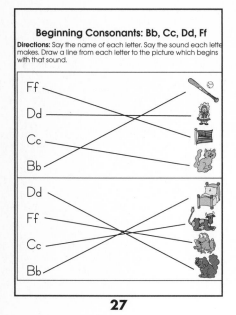

Beginning Consonants: Bb, Cc, Dd, Ff

Directions: Say the name of each letter. Say the sound each letter makes. Draw a line from each letter to the picture which begins with that sound.

27

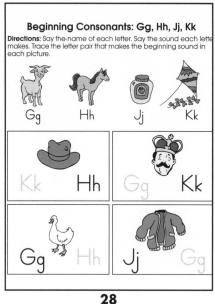

Beginning Consonants: Gg, Hh, Jj, Kk

Directions: Say the name of each letter. Say the sound each letter makes. Trace the letter pair that makes the beginning sound in each picture.

28

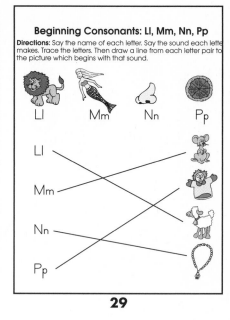

Beginning Consonants: Ll, Mm, Nn, Pp

Directions: Say the name of each letter. Say the sound each letter makes. Trace the letters. Then draw a line from each letter pair to the picture which begins with that sound.

29

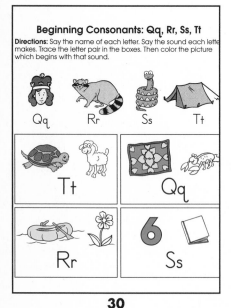

Beginning Consonants: Qq, Rr, Ss, Tt

Directions: Say the name of each letter. Say the sound each letter makes. Trace the letter pair in the boxes. Then color the picture which begins with that sound.

30

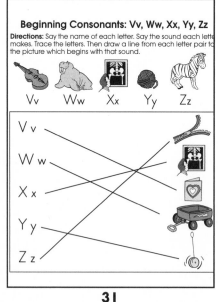

Beginning Consonants: Vv, Ww, Xx, Yy, Zz

Directions: Say the name of each letter. Say the sound each letter makes. Trace the letters. Then draw a line from each letter pair to the picture which begins with that sound.

31

Review

Directions: Help Meg, Kent and their dog, Sam, get to the magic castle. Trace each capital consonant letter and write the lower-case consonant next to it. Say the sound each consonant makes.

32

Review: Beginning Consonants

Directions: Say each picture name. Circle the letter that stands for the beginning sound.

Review: Beginning Consonants

Directions: Look at each picture. Say its name. Write the letter for the beginning sound in each picture.

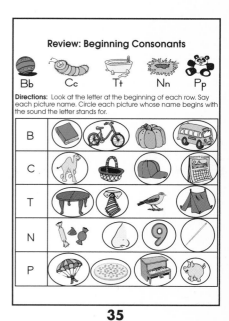

Review: Beginning Consonants

Directions: Look at the letter at the beginning of each row. Say each picture name. Circle each picture whose name begins with the sound the letter stands for.

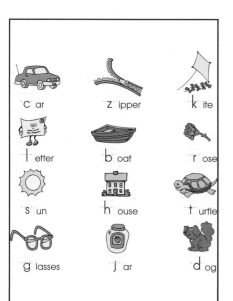

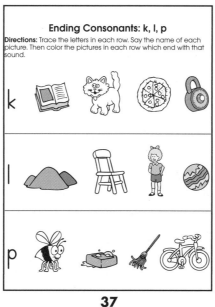

Ending Consonants: k, l, p

Directions: Trace the letters in each row. Say the name of each picture. Then color the pictures in each row which end with that sound.

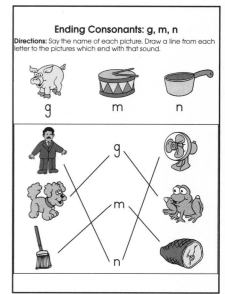

Ending Consonants: g, m, n

Directions: Say the name of each picture. Draw a line from each letter to the pictures which end with that sound.

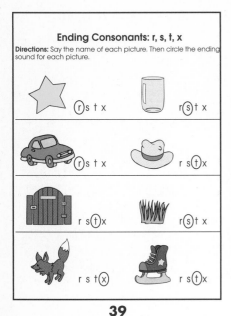

Ending Consonants: r, s, t, x

Directions: Say the name of each picture. Then circle the ending sound for each picture.

Ending Consonants

bed   bag   jam

Directions: Write the letter to complete each word.

ham   dad   rug

pig   dam   red

Beginning and Ending Consonants

Directions: Say the name of each picture. Write the beginning and ending sounds for each picture.

b ___ g   p ___ t
r ___ t   c ___ l
b ___ d   w ___ r
g ___ s   s ___ x

Beginning and Ending Consonants

Directions: Say the name of each picture. Draw a triangle around the letter that makes the **beginning** sound. Draw a square around the letter that makes the **ending** sound. Color the pictures.

o   t   f   d   v   t
x   r   t   g   a   k
l   m   x   g   p   t

Short Vowel Aa

Directions: Trace and write the letter Aa. Start at the dot. Say the sound the letter makes as you write it.

A A A A A A

a a a a a a

Directions: These pictures begin with the letter Aa. Color these pictures.

apple   ant

animals   astronaut

39   40   41

42   43   44

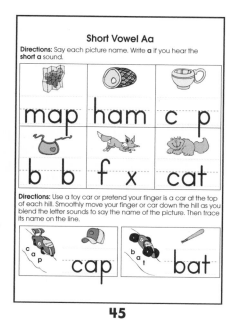

Short Vowel Aa

Directions: Say each picture name. Write **a** if you hear the **short a** sound.

map   ham   c p

b b   f x   cat

Directions: Use a toy car or pretend your finger is a car at the top of each hill. Smoothly move your finger or car down the hill as you blend the letter sounds to say the name of the picture. Then trace its name on the line.

cap   bat

45

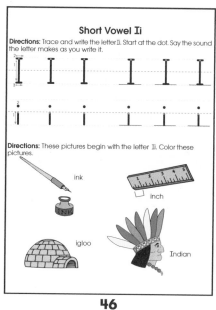

Short Vowel Ii

Directions: Trace and write the letter Ii. Start at the dot. Say the sound the letter makes as you write it.

I I I I I I

i i i i i i

Directions: These pictures begin with the letter Ii. Color these pictures.

ink

inch

igloo

Indian

46

Short Vowel Ii

Directions: Blend the letter sounds to read each word. Write the word on the line.

b i b   bib

p i n   pin

Directions: Write the word that names each picture. Then find three other things in the picture whose names have the short i sound and circle them.

bib

pin

47

Short Vowel Uu

Directions: Trace and write the letter Uu. Start at the dot. Say the sound the letter makes as you write it.

U U U U U U

u u u u u u

Directions: These pictures begin with the letter Uu. Color these pictures.

umbrella

up

under

umpire

48

Short Vowel Uu

Directions: Look at the pictures and read the words. Draw a line from each picture to the word that matches it.

bus   cup   gum   bug

49

Short Vowel Oo

Directions: Look at the pictures and read the words. Draw a line from each word to the picture which matches it.

sock   fox   log   dog

50

Phonics: Grade 1

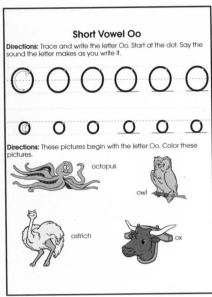

Short Vowel Oo

Directions: Trace and write the letter Oo. Start at the dot. Say the sound the letter makes as you write it.

O O O O O O

o o o o o o

Directions: These pictures begin with the letter Oo. Color these pictures.

octopus

owl

ostrich

ox

Short Vowel Ee

Directions: Trace and write the letter Ee. Start at the dot. Say the sound the letter makes as you write it.

E E E E E E

e e e e e e

Directions: These pictures begin with the letter Ee. Color these pictures.

elephant

eggs

envelope

elbow

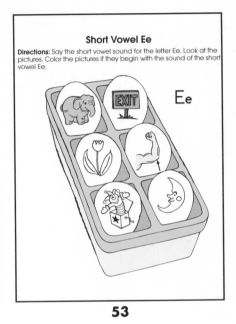

Short Vowel Ee

Directions: Say the short vowel sound for the letter Ee. Look at the pictures. Color the pictures if they begin with the sound of the short vowel Ee.

Ee

---

51   **52**   **53**

---

o u e   o u e   o u e

o u e   o u e   o u e

o u e   o u e   o u e

Short Vowels

Vowels are the letters **a, e, i, o** and **u**. Short **a** is the sound you hear in **ant**. Short **e** is the sound you hear in **elephant**. Short **i** is the sound you hear in **igloo**. Short **o** is the sound you hear in **octopus**. Short **u** is the sound you hear in **umbrella**.

Directions: Say the short vowel sound at the beginning of each row. Say the name of each picture. Then color the pictures which have the same short vowel sounds as that letter.

ă

ĕ

ĭ

ŏ

ŭ

Long Vowel Sounds

Directions: Write a, e, i, o or u in each blank to finish the word. Draw a line from the word to the picture.

c a ke

r o se

k i te

f ee t

m u le

---

54   **55**   **56**

57

58

59

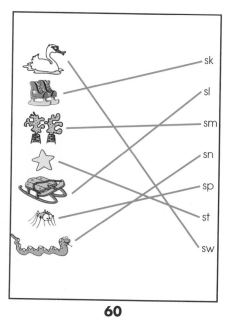

60

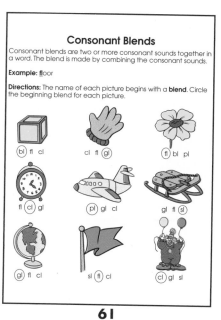

61

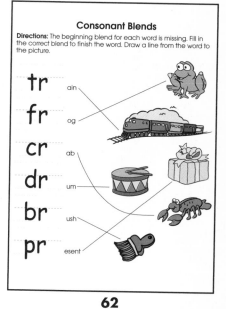

62

Phonics: Grade 1

Beginning Blends

Directions: Say the blend for each word as you search for it.

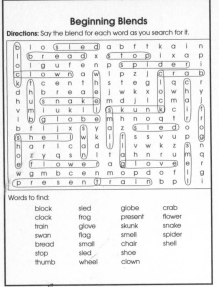

Words to find:

block	sled	globe	crab
clock	frog	present	flower
train	glove	skunk	snake
swan	flag	smell	spider
bread	small	chair	shell
stop	sled	shoe	
thumb	wheel	clown	

63

Consonant Blends

Directions: Look at the first picture in each row. Circle the pictures in the row that begin with the same sound.

chair

shell

thumb

wheel

64

be ___ lt

ra ___ ft

sa ___ lt

qui ___ lt

le ___ ft

65

Ending Consonant Blends

Directions: Every juke box has a word ending and a list of letters. Add each of the letters to the word ending to make rhyming words.

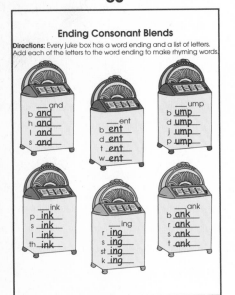

___ and
b **and**
h **and**
l **and**
s **and**

___ ent
b **ent**
d **ent**
t **ent**
w **ent**

___ ump
b **ump**
d **ump**
j **ump**
p **ump**

___ ink
p **ink**
s **ink**
l **ink**
th **ink**

___ ing
r **ing**
s **ing**
st **ing**
k **ing**

___ ank
b **ank**
r **ank**
s **ank**
t **ank**

66

Ending Consonant Blends

Directions: Draw a line from the picture to the blend that en the word.

lf

lk

sk

st

67

Ending Consonant Blends

Directions: Say the blend for each word as you search for it.

Words to find:

belt	raft	milk	shelf
mask	clasp	nest	band
think	went	lump	crank
ring	blank	shrink	land
bring	tent	dump	sing

68

Review

Directions: Finish each sentence with a word from the word box.

sting	shelf	drank	plant	stamp

1. Tom **drank** his milk.

2. A bee can **sting** you.

3. I put a **stamp** on my letter.

4. The **plant** is green.

5. The book is on the **shelf**

69

Phonics: Grade 1

80